BATS SET II

BUMBLEBEE BATS

Jill C. Wheeler
ABDO Publishing Company

visit us at
www.abdopub.com

Printed in the United States.

Cover Photo: © Merlin D. Tuttle, Bat Conservation International
Interior Photos: Animals Animals p. 13; Corbis p. 9; © Merlin D. Tuttle, Bat Conservation
    International pp. 5, 10-11, 17, 21; Peter Arnold p. 19

Series Coordinator: Tamara L. Britton
Editors: Tamara L. Britton, Stephanie Hedlund
Art Direction, Maps, and Diagrams: Neil Klinepier

Library of Congress Cataloging-in-Publication Data

Wheeler, Jill C., 1964-
    Bumblebee bats / Jill C. Wheeler.
        p. cm. -- (Bats. Set II)
    Includes bibliographical references and index.
    ISBN 1-59679-320-1
      1. Bumblebee bat--Juvenile literature. I. Title.

    QL737.C513W49 2005
    599.4--dc22
                                                            2005043273

CONTENTS

BUMBLEBEE BATS

There are more than 900 **species** of bats in the world. Only rodents have a larger number of species. Bats come in many different sizes. The bumblebee bat is the smallest bat of all. It is also the only species in its **family**.

This tiny bat got its name because it is about the size of a bumblebee. The bumblebee bat is also called Kitti's hog-nosed bat. It was named after biologist Kitti Thonglongya. He discovered the bats in 1973.

Bats are **mammals**. An amazing one-quarter of all mammals are bats. Humans are mammals, too. Bats and humans both have backbones. And, mother bats make milk for their babies, just like human mothers do. But, bats have a special **ability** that no other mammal has. They can fly!

Many people think bats are scary or harmful. This is not true. Bats are helpful to humans. They eat many insect pests. Some bats also help **pollinate** plants. They rarely harm humans or pets. Both bats and humans are important partners in Earth's **ecosystem**.

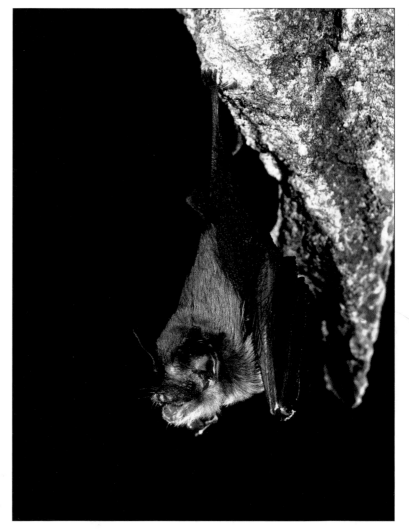

This bumblebee bat is roosting on a rock. Like all bats, bumblebee bats are part of the order Chiroptera. This is a Greek word that means "hand wing." Bats have hands that are also wings!

Where They're Found

Bats are found all around the world. They live everywhere except for some **isolated** islands and the North and South poles. But, bumblebee bats are only found in Sai Yok National Park in western Thailand.

Teak and bamboo grow in the park. These are popular woods for making furniture and other goods. So, many of the park's forests have been cut down. Clearing these forests destroys the bumblebee bat's **habitat**. It takes away the trees where they hunt for food.

Sai Yok's well-meaning tourists are hurting bumblebee bats, too. Some people try to see the tiny bats by creeping into the caves where the bats live. This disrupts the bats' sleep. They become too tired to go out and hunt. Then, they die of starvation.

All of these things have put bumblebee bats in danger of extinction. In fact, bumblebee bats are among the world's most **endangered species**. To save the bats, Thailand's government passed laws in 1981 to protect them from hunting and trade.

THAILAND

Sai Yok
National
Park

N

WHERE THEY LIVE

Bumblebee bats live in limestone caves in Sai Yok National Park. The park is in Kanchanaburi **province**. In the park, evergreen trees grow near bamboo forests. Teak trees grow along the Kwai River.

Like all bats, bumblebee bats are **nocturnal**. They spend their days **roosting** in warm caves. They like to be far from people and other animals. So, they roost as deep in the caves as they can.

There may be 10 to 15 bats in a cave. Yet the bats do not cluster together. They roost a little ways apart from each other.

At dusk, the bumblebee bats leave their caves to hunt. Their favorite hunting grounds are bamboo clumps and the branches of teak trees. After they eat, the bats return to their roost. They go out just before dawn and eat some more. Then, they come back to sleep all day.

Sai Yok National Park was created for the bumblebee bat. It is also famous for its many waterfalls, such as this one on the Kwai River.

SIZES

The tiny bumblebee bat is only about one to one and a half inches (2.5 to 4 cm) long. Their **wingspan** is just over five inches (13 cm). They weigh only seven one-hundredths of an ounce (2 g). That is only about as heavy as a dime!

Compare that to the flying fox bat. Some **species** of flying foxes are more than 15 inches (38 cm) long. They can have a wingspan of more than 5 feet (1.5 m)! These are the world's largest flying **mammals**.

Bumblebee bats are the smallest bats in the world.

SHAPES

Bumblebee bats are soft and furry. The fur on their backs is usually brown, reddish, or gray colored. On their sides, the fur is a lighter color. The fur hides their small eyes. For such a small bat, their ears are quite large! And, their little nose looks like a pig's snout. That is why they are also called hog-nosed bats!

Bumblebee bats have arms and hands, like humans do. Each hand has four long fingers, and a thumb with a claw. Their wings, or flight **membranes**, are dark brown. These membranes stretch between their fingers, body, and legs. Their wings have a special tip that helps them hover in the air when hunting. They do not have a tail.

A bumblebee bat's knees bend backward. This allows them to **roost** easily on cave ceilings. Their hind feet are long and narrow. When the bat is roosting, the weight of its body pulling down on the legs locks its toes into position on uneven surfaces.

The bumblebee bat's unusually shaped nose is not uncommon in the bat world. Many bats have odd-looking faces. This is because of the special way most bat **species** find their way around and locate food.

Bat Anatomy

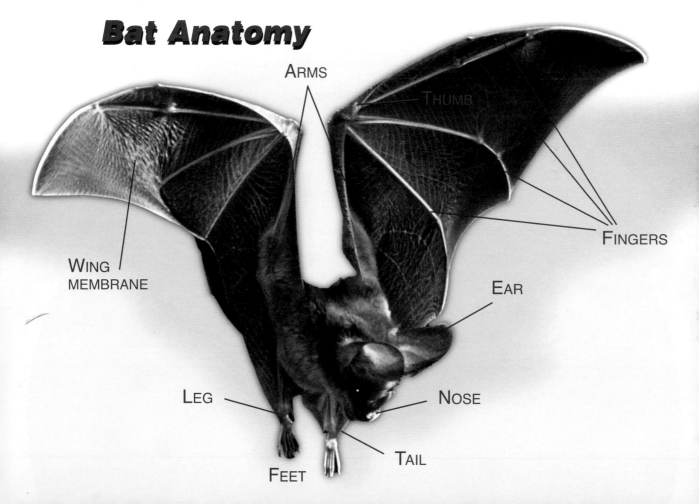

ARMS

THUMB

FINGERS

WING MEMBRANE

EAR

LEG

NOSE

FEET

TAIL

SENSES

You may have heard the phrase "blind as a bat." This rumor probably started because bats only come out at night. Yet bats can see. They can also hear, smell, taste, and feel. About half of all bats have another sense called echolocation. This is how bats "see" in the dark.

To use echolocation, bats make high-pitched sounds. Some bats make these sounds from their throat, and some from their nose. These sound waves go out and bounce off an object such as a tree, building, or insect.

The echo of the sound returns to the bat. It catches the echoes in its large ears. The bat uses the echo to locate an object. The echoes also tell bats how big the object is.

Humans can't hear the sounds bats make. But, the bats can hear them well! Bats use echolocation to fly safely and to find food. They also use echolocation to avoid danger.

Sound wave sent out by bat

Echo wave received by bat

DEFENSE

The bumblebee bat's small size makes it a bite-sized snack for many **predators**. Bats make tasty meals for hawks and other birds of **prey**. Some snakes and frogs like eating them, too.

Bumblebee bats avoid some predators by only going out at night. However, predators can be quite smart. Some wait outside the cave and try to catch bats as they fly back into their home in the morning. The bats use echolocation to avoid these predators.

When the bumblebee bats enter their cave, they **roost** far off the ground near other bats. This roosting pattern helps the bats avoid the predators that sneak into their caves. If a predator approaches, the bats alert each other. Since they are all hanging upside down, it is easy for them to drop down and quickly fly away.

The bumblebee bat's ability for quick flight helps the tiny bat stay safe from its many enemies.

FOOD

Bumblebee bats are **prey** for hungry **predators**. But, they are also predators themselves. Bumblebee bats eat insects and spiders. They find them around the tops of trees. They can hover in the air to catch their food if necessary. Or, they can fly after it and catch it in their wings. For this, they have a special flap of skin behind their wings.

Bats can catch an amazing number of insects each night. The tiny pipistrelle bat is slightly larger than the bumblebee bat. However, it can eat more than 2,000 insects a night. Larger bats can eat even more bugs. Some northern bats have been found to eat 1,000 mosquitoes per hour.

Their big appetite makes the little bumblebee bat an important part of the **ecosystem**. They help humans by reducing the number of insect pests.

To eat all those insects, the pipistrelle bat often leaves the roost before sunset. And, it can go out to eat more than once a night.

BABIES

To continue to keep the **ecosystem** healthy, bumblebee bats need a safe place to reproduce. Bumblebee bats **roost** far back in their caves. And, they fly away when **disturbed**. So, researchers do not know much about how bumblebee bats mate and raise their babies.

However, scientists think bumblebee bats are a lot like other bat **species**. After mating, male bats leave the females. They do not stay to help with the babies. Female bats roost together, and have babies in large communities. Since bats are **mammals**, their babies are born alive.

Bats babies are called pups. Most bats have only one or sometimes two pups a year. Bat pups are born fairly well developed. This gives them a better chance of surviving.

Mother bats feed their pups with milk. After about six weeks, bumblebee bat pups can live on their own. Then, they become part of the **ecosystem**, and the process begins again.

Mother bats usually leave their pups while they go out and hunt. When they return, they find their pup by its special smell and squeak sound.

Glossary

ability - to have the power to do something.

disturb - to interrupt or break in upon.

ecosystem (EE-koh-sihs-tuhm) - a community of organisms and their environment.

endangered - in danger of becoming extinct.

family - a group that scientists use to classify similar plants or animals. It ranks above a genus and below an order.

habitat - a place where a living thing is naturally found.

isolate - to separate from something.

mammal - an animal with a backbone that nurses its young with milk.

membrane - a thin, easily bent layer of animal tissue.

nocturnal (nahk-TUHR-nuhl) - active at night.

order - a group that scientists use to classify similar plants or animals. It ranks above a family and below a class.

pollinate - when birds and insects transfer pollen from one flower or plant to another.

predator - an animal that kills and eats other animals.

prey - animals that are eaten by other animals; also the act of seizing prey.

province - a geographical or governmental division of a country.

roost - a place, such as a cave or a tree, where bats rest during the day; also, to perch.

species (SPEE-sheez) - a kind or type.

wingspan - the distance from one wing-tip to the other when the wings are spread.

WEB SITES

To learn more about bumblebee bats, visit ABDO Publishing Company on the World Wide Web at **www.abdopub.com**. Web sites about bats are featured on our Book Links page. These links are routinely monitored and updated to provide the most current information available.

INDEX